*Selected Prose of Robert Frost*

# SELECTED PROSE

*Edited by Hyde Cox and Edward Connery Lathem*

# OF ROBERT FROST

*Holt, Rinehart and Winston: New York, Chicago, San Francisco*

Library of Congress Catalog Card Number: 66–10268

First Edition

Grateful acknowledgment is extended to the following for permission to include material which first appeared in their publications:
*The Amherst Student*, Amherst College, for the letter which appeared in the March 25, 1935, issue of *The Amherst Student*. All Rights Reserved.
Jonathan Cape Limited, London, for "A Romantic Chasm," the Introduction to the English edition of *A Masque of Reason*. All Rights Reserved.
*The Christian Science Monitor*, Boston, for "Poetry of Amy Lowell," which first appeared in *The Christian Science Monitor* and also in *Robert Frost: The Trial by Existence*, by Elizabeth Shepley Sergeant, copyright © 1960 by Elizabeth Shepley Sergeant.
The Dial Press, Inc., New York, New York, for the Preface to *Memoirs of the Notorious Stephen Burroughs*, copyright, 1924 by The Dial Press, Inc. All Rights Reserved.
Helen Hartness Flanders, for "The Hear-Say Ballad," the Introduction to *Ballads Migrant in New England*, copyright, 1953 by Helen Hartness Flanders. All Rights Reserved.
Holt, Rinehart and Winston, Inc., New York, New York, for the Preface to Robert Frost's play, *A Way Out*, copyright 1917, 1929 by Robert Frost, from *Robert Frost: The Trial by Existence*, by Elizabeth Shepley Sergeant, copyright © 1960 by Elizabeth Shepley Sergeant; for "The Figure a Poem Makes" from *Complete Poems of Robert Frost*, copyright 1949 by Holt, Rinehart and Winston, Inc.; and for "The Prerequisites," which appeared as the Preface to Robert Frost's collection, *Aforesaid*, copyright, 1954 by Holt, Rinehart and Winston, Inc.
The Macmillan Company, New York, New York, for the Introduction to *King Jasper* by E. A. Robinson, copyright 1935 © 1963 by The Macmillan Company.
The National Institute of Arts and Letters, New York, New York, for the speech delivered before the Institute in 1939 and printed in the *National Institute of Arts and Letters News Bulletin*, Volume 5, 1939. All Rights Reserved.
Time, Inc., New York, New York, for "Perfect Day—A Day of Prowess," which appeared first in the July 23, 1956, issue of *Sports Illustrated*, copyright © 1956 by The Estate of Robert Frost.
The World Publishing Company, Cleveland and New York, for "Maturity No Object," the Introduction to *New Poets of England and America*, an Anthology edited and selected by Donald Hall, Robert Pack, and Louis Simpson, a Meridian Book. Copyright © 1957 by The World Publishing Company.

81565–0116
Printed in the United States of America

# CONTENTS

# Introduction

MORE than once in the later years of his life Robert Frost was urged to publish a selection of his prose. His prefaces to his own and to a few other books were available only separately; and occasional pieces he had written, although known to some, had never been gathered together in a book and were, therefore, not readily available to the ever-growing number of people for whom they would have had meaning.

In a letter in 1945 he wrote, "I plan prose and I promise prose but with no very sincere belief that I will do it at any particular time." He was entirely willing to stand on his statement, "The utmost of ambition is to lodge a few poems where they will be hard to get rid of. . . ." No one is likely to forget that he was first and always the poet. Yet he was also a masterful writer of prose. "The speaking tone of voice somehow entangled in the words" is evident in his prose as it is in his verse.

One critic has aptly remembered, in writing about Frost, Dryden's phrase "the other harmony of prose," and Frost himself once referred to prose as "my other mood." His other mood was almost always the result of a necessity: the need to write a preface or to acknowledge an honor or to honor someone else; and Frost, like all great performers, rose to occasions, adapting

7

his prose to the nature of the need. Several voices can be heard in his prose, and these voices are all represented in this book. There is a variety among the pieces themselves. They cover such different subjects as poetry, baseball, and religion. But the voices of the writer vary within the pieces, as well as between them. There is the voice of the teacher, of the philosopher, of the friend, and—most often—of the maker of great figures of speech.

Whatever Mr. Frost had to say in his latter years—in print or on the platform, in verse or prose—was welcomed by thousands of admirers. He made no secret of his passionate preference for his own country; but his words reached other countries than his own, almost in spite of himself. Near the end of his long life his countrymen showed that they appreciated his partiality, and he became a very popular national figure.

He was able in these years, as many had reason to know, to be the friend of friends to a variety of people and to show at the same time an almost excessive concern about his country's problems and the part he might even play as a statesman—a role which naturally he never thought entirely beyond the reach of a poet.

There were in his very old age several reasons why he never got around to publishing his prose or authorizing anyone else to do it. In the role of celebrity he was beset with invitations to speak and to play a part in affairs, and his increasing enjoyment of these activities left him with little inclination to concentrate on a book of prose. Also, the bulk of what might have been included in such a volume continued to increase, chiefly because during the last ten years of his life he was more and more regularly recorded when he spoke in public. Most of these talks preserved on tape or by other means were of such interest that they became eligible for inclusion in any collection. He was aware that many people felt that way, but he kept postponing the project. He was more interested in the growth of his metaphors than in bringing them to book.

His statements on poetry and on what are called "great issues" were continually changing and growing. Great issues were among the things he loved most and lived with most intimately. You couldn't have breakfast with him without running into great issues—much less take a midnight walk around the streets of one of the many towns he haunts: Amherst or Hanover, Cambridge or Key West. . . .

It was his addiction to playing with great issues that made one hang on his words. It was that, but it was more than that. His serious biographers forever will have to try to explain the extraordinary impact of his personality on almost all the people who heard him talk, and most of all on those who conversed with him. "I'm not a monologist, you know," he would say; but so stimulating was the quality of his never-ending conversation that even two or three by a fireside were happy to let conversation turn into monologue. With a crowd he was ready (as a high-pressure area always is) to move into low-pressure areas. Like weather, he came in variously: sometimes suddenly like a storm, sometimes gently. But he seldom failed to change the climate when he moved in.

His poetry will outlast his voice and presence, and poetry is what he chose to be remembered by. It is his formal statement. When anyone asked him the meaning of one of his poems, he would reply, "What do you want me to do, say it again in different and less good words?" Prose was for him an informality. Except for letters, he wrote very little prose in the course of his career. But his prose illuminates both his poetry and his character.

"I don't like to read about a man," Frost often said. "I'd rather read the man himself."

The editors of this volume were both his intimate friends and knew him well enough to write a book about him, but remembering his preference—and sharing it—have chosen instead to present the man himself, as his prose reveals him.

We have not tried to anticipate the day when every scrap of his prose will be collected; we are not editing the complete prose of Robert Frost, although none of the pieces we have omitted from any period in his career was without attraction. We are not here concerned with his letters or with the handful of plays he attempted; and we have not included his recorded public talks, which deserve to be published separately. We have included in this first prose book only pieces that appeared in his lifetime, three of which began as talks but are included because they were edited and approved by him. Everything selected is printed in full, as originally published, without alterations or omissions.

Robert Frost is reported to have said many years ago, in conversation with a student, "I suppose that someday when I'm about ninety I'll begin to write prose." As it turned out, he did not. We have chosen, therefore, from all the prose that does exist what we think Mr. Frost himself might have chosen in the last year of his life—when he was about ninety—if he had not kept such a zest for living that he hadn't time to be a collector of himself.

HYDE COX

EDWARD CONNERY LATHEM

*Preface to* A Way Out

# Preface to *A Way Out*

[E]VERYTHING written is
as good as it is dramatic. It
need not declare itself in form, but it is drama or nothing. A
least lyric alone may have a hard time, but it can make a beginning, and lyric will be piled on lyric till all are easily heard as
sung or spoken by a person in a scene—in character, in a setting.
By whom, where and when is the question. By a dreamer of
the better world out in a storm in autumn; by a lover under a
window at night. It is the same with the essay. It may manage
alone or it may take unto itself other essays for help, but it must
make itself heard as by Stevenson on an island, or Lamb in
London.

A dramatic necessity goes deep into the nature of the sentence. Sentences are not different enough to hold the attention
unless they are dramatic. No ingenuity of varying structure
will do. All that can save them is the speaking tone of voice
somehow entangled in the words and fastened to the page for

---

Of the fifteen selections in this book, the earliest appeared in 1924 and the
most recent in 1959. They are not, however, arranged here in chronological
order. The first is the preface to Mr. Frost's little play *A Way Out*, as published
in 1929. Except for its last sentence, this statement might stand as a preface to
all of the poet's beliefs about the art of writing.

13

the ear of the imagination. That is all that can save poetry from sing-song, all that can save prose from itself.

I have always come as near the dramatic as I could this side of actually writing a play. Here for once I have written a play without (as I should like to believe) having gone very far from where I have spent my life.

*"The Figure a Poem Makes"*

# "The Figure a Poem Makes"

ABSTRACTION is an old story with the philosophers, but it has been like a new toy in the hands of the artists of our day. Why can't we have any one quality of poetry we choose by itself? We can have in thought. Then it will go hard if we can't in practice. Our lives for it.

Granted no one but a humanist much cares how sound a poem is if it is only *a* sound. The sound is the gold in the ore. Then we will have the sound out alone and dispense with the inessential. We do till we make the discovery that the object in writing poetry is to make all poems sound as different as possible from each other, and the resources for that of vowels, consonants, punctuation, syntax, words, sentences, meter are not enough. We need the help of context—meaning—subject matter. That is the greatest help towards variety. All that can be done with words is soon told. So also with meters—particularly in our language where there are virtually but two, strict

---

"The Figure a Poem Makes" is probably the best known of Mr. Frost's prose pieces, because it has since 1939 been printed and reprinted as the introduction to editions of his collected poems. It is characteristic both in tone of voice and in the way he plays around the edges of his subject with politics and religion. It contains some of his most memorable figures of speech.

iambic and loose iambic. The ancients with many were still poor if they depended on meters for all tune. It is painful to watch our sprung-rhythmists straining at the point of omitting one short from a foot for relief from monotony. The possibilities for tune from the dramatic tones of meaning struck across the rigidity of a limited meter are endless. And we are back in poetry as merely one more art of having something to say, sound or unsound. Probably better if sound, because deeper and from wider experience.

Then there is this wildness whereof it is spoken. Granted again that it has an equal claim with sound to being a poem's better half. If it is a wild tune, it is a poem. Our problem then is, as modern abstractionists, to have the wildness pure; to be wild with nothing to be wild about. We bring up as aberrationists, giving way to undirected associations and kicking ourselves from one chance suggestion to another in all directions as of a hot afternoon in the life of a grasshopper. Theme alone can steady us down. Just as the first mystery was how a poem could have a tune in such a straightness as meter, so the second mystery is how a poem can have wildness and at the same time a subject that shall be fulfilled.

It should be of the pleasure of a poem itself to tell how it can. The figure a poem makes. It begins in delight and ends in wisdom. The figure is the same as for love. No one can really hold that the ecstasy should be static and stand still in one place. It begins in delight, it inclines to the impulse, it assumes direction with the first line laid down, it runs a course of lucky events, and ends in a clarification of life—not necessarily a great clarification, such as sects and cults are founded on, but in a momentary stay against confusion. It has denouement. It has an outcome that though unforeseen was predestined from the first image of the original mood—and indeed from the very mood.

It is but a trick poem and no poem at all if the best of it was thought of first and saved for the last. It finds its own name as it goes and discovers the best waiting for it in some final phrase at once wise and sad—the happy-sad blend of the drinking song. No tears in the writer, no tears in the reader. No surprise for the writer, no surprise for the reader. For me the initial delight is in the surprise of remembering something I didn't know I knew. I am in a place, in a situation, as if I had materialized from cloud or risen out of the ground. There is a glad recognition of the long lost and the rest follows. Step by step the wonder of unexpected supply keeps growing. The impressions most useful to my purpose seem always those I was unaware of and so made no note of at the time when taken, and the conclusion is come to that like giants we are always hurling experience ahead of us to pave the future with against the day when we may want to strike a line of purpose across it for somewhere. The line will have the more charm for not being mechanically straight. We enjoy the straight crookedness of a good walking stick. Modern instruments of precision are being used to make things crooked as if by eye and hand in the old days.

I tell how there may be a better wildness of logic than of inconsequence. But the logic is backward, in retrospect, after the act. It must be more felt than seen ahead like prophecy. It must be a revelation, or a series of revelations, as much for the poet as for the reader. For it to be that there must have been the greatest freedom of the material to move about in it and to establish relations in it regardless of time and space, previous relation, and everything but affinity. We prate of freedom. We call our schools free because we are not free to stay away from them till we are sixteen years of age. I have given up my democratic prejudices and now willingly set the lower classes free to be completely taken care of by the upper classes. Political freedom is nothing to me. I bestow it right and left. All I would keep for myself is the freedom of my material—the condition of body and mind now and then to summons aptly from the vast chaos of all I have lived through.

Scholars and artists thrown together are often annoyed at the puzzle of where they differ. Both work from knowledge; but I suspect they differ most importantly in the way their knowledge is come by. Scholars get theirs with conscientious thoroughness along projected lines of logic; poets theirs cavalierly and as it happens in and out of books. They stick to nothing deliberately, but let what will stick to them like burrs where they walk in the fields. No acquirement is on assignment, or even self-assignment. Knowledge of the second kind is much more available in the wild free ways of wit and art. A school boy may be defined as one who can tell you what he knows in the order in which he learned it. The artist must value himself as he snatches a thing from some previous order in time and space into a new order with not so much as a ligature clinging to it of the old place where it was organic.

More than once I should have lost my soul to radicalism if it had been the originality it was mistaken for by its young converts. Originality and initiative are what I ask for my country. For myself the originality need be no more than the freshness of a poem run in the way I have described: from delight to wisdom. The figure is the same as for love. Like a piece of ice on a hot stove the poem must ride on its own melting. A poem may be worked over once it is in being, but may not be worried into being. Its most precious quality will remain its having run itself and carried away the poet with it. Read it a hundred times: it will forever keep its freshness as a metal keeps its fragrance. It can never lose its sense of a meaning that once unfolded by surprise as it went.

*"The Constant Symbol"*

# "The Constant Symbol"

THERE seems to be some such folk saying as that easy to understand is contemptible, hard to understand irritating. The implication is that just easy enough, just hard enough, right in the middle, is what literary criticism ought to foster. A glance backward over the past convinces me otherwise. The *Iliad*, *Odyssey*, and *Aeneid* are easy. The *Purgatorio* is said to be hard. The Song of Songs *is* hard. There have been works lately to surpass all records for hardness. Some knotted riddles tell what may be worth our trouble. But hard or easy seems to me of slight use as a test either way.

Texture is surely something. A good piece of weaving takes rank with a picture as decoration for the wall of a studio, though it must be admitted to verge on the arty. There is a time of apprenticeship to texture when it shouldn't matter if the stuff is never made up into anything. There may be scraps of repeated form all over it. But form as a whole! Don't be shocking! The title of his first book was *Fragments*. The artist has to grow up

"The Constant Symbol" was first published in *The Atlantic Monthly* in October 1946. Later in the same year it appeared as the introductory essay to the Modern Library edition of Mr. Frost's poems.

and coarsen a little before he looks on texture as not an end in itself.

There are many other things I have found myself saying about poetry, but the chiefest of these is that it is metaphor, saying one thing and meaning another, saying one thing in terms of another, the pleasure of ulteriority. Poetry is simply made of metaphor. So also is philosophy—and science, too, for that matter, if it will take the soft impeachment from a friend. Every poem is a new metaphor inside or it is nothing. And there is a sense in which all poems are the same old metaphor always.

Every single poem written regular is a symbol small or great of the way the will has to pitch into commitments deeper and deeper to a rounded conclusion and then be judged for whether any original intention it had has been strongly spent or weakly lost; be it in art, politics, school, church, business, love, or marriage—in a piece of work or in a career. Strongly spent is synonymous with kept.

We may speak after sentence, resenting judgment. How can the world know anything so intimate as what we were intending to do? The answer is the world presumes to know. The ruling passion in man is not as Viennese as is claimed. It is rather a gregarious instinct to keep together by minding each other's business. Grex rather than sex. We *must* be preserved from becoming egregious. The beauty of socialism is that it will end the individuality that is always crying out mind your own business. Terence's answer would be all human business is my business. No more invisible means of support, no more invisible motives, no more invisible anything. The ultimate commitment is giving in to it that an outsider may see what we were up to sooner and better than we ourselves. The bard has said in effect, Unto these forms did I commend the spirit. It may take him a year after the act to confess he only betrayed the spirit with a rhymster's cleverness and to forgive his enemies the critics for not having listened to his oaths and protestations to the contrary. Had he anything to be true to? Was he true to it? Did he use good words? You couldn't tell unless you made out what idea they were supposed to be good for. Every poem is an epitome of the great predicament; a figure of the will braving alien entanglements.

Take the President in the White House. A study of the success of his intention might have to go clear back to when as a young politician, youthfully step-careless, he made the choice between the two parties of our system. He may have stood for a moment wishing he knew of a third party nearer the ideal; but only for a moment, since he was practical. And in fact he may have been so little impressed with the importance of his choice that he left his first commitment to be made for him by his friends and relatives. It was only a small commitment anyway, like a kiss. He can scarcely remember how much credit he deserved personally for the decision it took. Calculation is usually no part in the first step in any walk. And behold him now a statesman so multifariously closed in on with obligations and answerabilities that sometimes he loses his august temper. He might as well have got himself into a sestina royal.

Or he may be a religious nature who lightly gets committed to a nameable church through an older friend in plays and games at the Y.M.C.A. The next he knows he is in a theological school and next in the pulpit of a Sunday wrestling with the angel for a blessing on his self-defensive interpretation of the Creed. What of his original intention now? At least he has had the advantage of having it more in his heart than in his head; so that he should have made shift to assert it without being chargeable with compromise. He could go a long way before he had

to declare anything he could be held to. He began with freedom
to squander. He has to acknowledge himself in a tighter and
tighter place. But his courage asked for it. It would have been
the same if he had gone to the North Pole or climbed Everest.
All that concerns *us* is whether his story was one of conform-
ance or performance.

There's an indulgent smile I get for the recklessness of the
unnecessary commitment I made when I came to the first line
in the second stanza of a poem in this book called "Stopping by
Woods on a Snowy Evening." I was riding too high to care
what trouble I incurred. And it was all right so long as I didn't
suffer deflection.

The poet goes in like a rope skipper to make the most of his
opportunities. If he trips himself he stops the rope. He is of our
stock and has been brought up by ear to choice of two metres,
strict iambic and loose iambic (not to count varieties of the
latter). He may have any length of line up to six feet. He may
use an assortment of line lengths for any shape of stanza like
Herrick in "To Daffodils." Not that he is running wild. His intention is of course a particular mood that won't be satisfied
with anything less than its own fulfillment. But it is not yet a
thought concerned with what becomes it. One thing to know
it by: it shrinks shyly from anticipatory expression. Tell love
beforehand and, as Blake says, it loses flow without filling the
mould; the cast will be a reject. The freshness of a poem belongs
absolutely to its not having been thought out and then set to
verse as the verse in turn might be set to music. A poem is the
emotion of having a thought while the reader waits a little anx-
iously for the success of dawn. The only discipline to begin with
is the inner mood that at worst may give the poet a false start or
two like the almost microscopic filament of cotton that goes
before the blunt thread-end and must be picked up first by the
eye of the needle. He must be entranced to the exact premoni-

tion. No mystery is meant. When familiar friends approach
each other in the street both are apt to have this experience in
feeling before knowing the pleasantry they will inflict on each
other in passing.

Probably there is something between the mood and the vocal
imagination (images of the voice speaking) that determines a
man's first commitment to metre and length of line.

Suppose him to have written down "When in disgrace with
Fortune and men's eyes." He has uttered about as much as he
has to live up to in the theme as in the form. Odd how the
two advance into the open pari passu. He has given out that he
will descend into Hades, but he has confided in no one how far
before he will turn back, or whether he will turn back at all,
and by what jutting points of rock he will pick his way. He may
proceed as in blank verse. Two lines more, however, and he has
let himself in for rhyme, three more and he has set himself a
stanza. Up to this point his discipline has been the self-discipline
whereof it is written in so great praise. The harsher discipline
from without is now well begun. He who knows not both
knows neither. His worldly commitments are now three or
four deep. Between us, he was no doubt bent on the sonnet in
the first place from habit, and what's the use in pretending he
was a freer agent than he had any ambition to be? He had made
most of his commitments all in one plunge. The only suspense
he asks us to share with him is in the theme. He goes down, for
instance, to a depth that must surprise him as much as it does us.
But he doesn't even have the say of how long his piece will be.
Any worry is as to whether he will outlast or last out the four-
teen lines—have to cramp or stretch to come out even—have
enough bread for the butter or butter for the bread. As a matter
of fact, he gets through in twelve lines and doesn't know quite
what to do with the last two.

Things like that and worse are the reason the sonnet is so suspect a form and has driven so many to free verse and even to the novel. Many a quatrain is salvaged from a sonnet that went agley. Dobson confesses frankly to having changed from one form to another after starting: "I intended an Ode and it turned to a Sonnet." But he reverses the usual order of being driven from the harder down to the easier. And he has a better excuse for weakness of will than most, namely, Rose.

Jeremiah, it seems, has had his sincerity questioned because the anguish of his lamentations was tamable to the form of twenty-two stanzas for the twenty-two letters of the alphabet. The Hebrew alphabet has been kept to the twenty-two letters it came out of Egypt with, so the number twenty-two means as much form as ever.

But there they go again with the old doubt about law and order. (The communist looks forward to a day of order without law, bless his merciful heart.) To the right person it must seem naive to distrust form as such. The very words of the dictionary are a restriction to make the best of or stay out of and be silent. Coining new words isn't encouraged. We play the words as we find them. We make them do. Form in language is such a disjected lot of old broken pieces it seems almost as non-existent as the spirit till the two embrace in the sky. They are not to be thought of as encountering in rivalry but in creation. No judgment on either alone counts. We see what Whitman's extravagance may have meant when he said the body was the soul.

Here is where it all comes out. The mind is a baby giant who, more provident in the cradle than he knows, has hurled his paths in life all round ahead of him like playthings given—data so-called. They are vocabulary, grammar, prosody, and diary, and it will go hard if he can't find stepping stones of them for his feet wherever he wants to go. The way will be zigzag, but it will be a straight crookedness like the walking stick he cuts himself in the bushes for an emblem. He will be judged as he does or doesn't let this zig or that zag project him off out of his general direction.

Teacher or student or investigator whose chance on these defenseless lines may seize, your pardon if for once I point you out what ordinarily you would point me out. To some it will seem strange that I have written my verse regular all this time without knowing till yesterday that it was from fascination with this constant symbol I celebrate. To the right person it will seem lucky; since in finding out too much too soon there is danger of arrest. Does anyone believe I would have committed myself to the treason-reason-season rhyme-set in my "Reluctance" if I had been blasé enough to know that these three words about exhausted the possibilities? No rhyming dictionary for me to make me face the facts of rhyme. I may say the strain of rhyming is less since I came to see words as phrase-ends to countless phrases just as the syllables ly, ing, and ation are word-ends to countless words. Leave something to learn later. We'd have lost most of our innocence by forty anyway even if we never went to school a day.

*"Education by Poetry"*

# "Education by Poetry"

I AM going to urge nothing in my talk. I am not an advocate. I am going to consider a matter, and commit a description. And I am going to describe other colleges than Amherst. Or, rather say all that is good can be taken as about Amherst; all that is bad will be about other colleges.

I know whole colleges where all American poetry is barred—whole colleges. I know whole colleges where all contemporary poetry is barred.

I once heard of a minister who turned his daughter—his poetry-writing daughter—out on the street to earn a living, because he said there should be no more books written; God wrote one book, and that was enough. (My friend George Russell, "Æ", has read no literature, he protests, since just before Chaucer.)

That all seems sufficiently safe, and you can say one thing for it. It takes the onus off the poetry of having to be used to teach

"Education by Poetry" was a talk delivered at Amherst College and subsequently revised for publication in the *Amherst Graduates' Quarterly* of February 1931. It is from the conclusion of this piece that Mr. Frost once extracted the text separately printed under the title *The Four Beliefs*.

children anything. It comes pretty hard on poetry, I sometimes think,—what it has to bear in the teaching process.

Then I know whole colleges where, though they let in older poetry, they manage to bar all that is poetical in it by treating it as something other than poetry. It is not so hard to do that. Their reason I have often hunted for. It may be that these people act from a kind of modesty. Who are professors that they should attempt to deal with a thing as high and as fine as poetry? Who are *they*? There is a certain manly modesty in that.

That is the best general way of settling the problem; treat all poetry as if it were something else than poetry, as if it were syntax, language, science. Then you can even come down into the American and into the contemporary without any special risk.

There is another reason they have, and that is that they are, first and foremost in life, markers. They have the marking problem to consider. Now, I stand here a teacher of many years' experience and I have never complained of having had to mark. I had rather mark anyone for anything—for his looks, carriage, his ideas, his correctness, his exactness, anything you please,—I would rather give him a mark in terms of letters, A, B, C, D, than have to use adjectives on him. We are all being marked by each other all the time, classified, ranked, put in our place, and I see no escape from that. I am no sentimentalist. You have got to mark, and you have got to mark, first of all, for accuracy, for correctness. But if I am going to give a mark, that is the least part of my marking. The hard part is the part beyond that, the part where the adventure begins.

One other way to rid the curriculum of the poetry nuisance has been considered. More merciful than the others it would neither abolish nor denature the poetry, but only turn it out to disport itself, with the plays and games—in no wise discredited, though given no credit for. Any one who liked to teach poetically could take his subject, whether English, Latin, Greek or French, out into the nowhere along with the poetry. One side of a sharp line would be left to the rigorous and righteous; the other side would be assigned to the flowery where they would know what could be expected of them. Grade marks where more easily given, of course, in the courses concentrating on correctness and exactness as the only forms of honesty recognized by plain people; a general indefinite mark of $X$ in the courses that scatter brains over taste and opinion. On inquiry I have found no teacher willing to take position on either side of the line, either among the rigors or among the flowers. No one is willing to admit that his discipline is not partly in exactness. No one is willing to admit that his discipline is not partly in taste and enthusiasm.

How shall a man go through college without having been marked for taste and judgment? What will become of him? What will his end be? He will have to take continuation courses for college graduates. He will have to go to night schools. They are having night schools now, you know, for college graduates. Why? Because they have not been educated enough to find their way around in contemporary literature. They don't know what they may safely like in the libraries and galleries. They don't know how to judge an editorial when they see one. They don't know how to judge a political campaign. They don't know when they are being fooled by a metaphor, an analogy, a parable. And metaphor is, of course, what we are talking about. Education by poetry is education by metaphor.

Suppose we stop short of imagination, initiative, enthusiasm, inspiration and originality—dread words. Suppose we don't mark in such things at all. There are still two minimal things, that we have got to take care of, taste and judgment. Americans

are supposed to have more judgment than taste, but taste is
there to be dealt with. That is what poetry, the only art in the
colleges of arts, is there for. I for my part would not be afraid to
go in for enthusiasm. There is the enthusiasm like a blinding
light, or the enthusiasm of the deafening shout, the crude enthusiasm that you get uneducated by poetry, outside of poetry.
It is exemplified in what I might call "sunset raving." You look
westward toward the sunset, or if you get up early enough,
eastward toward the sunrise, and you rave. It is oh's and ah's
with you and no more.

But the enthusiasm I mean is taken through the prism of the
intellect and spread on the screen in a color, all the way from
hyperbole at one end—or overstatement, at one end—to understatement at the other end. It is a long strip of dark lines and
many colors. Such enthusiasm is one object of all teaching in
poetry. I heard wonderful things said about Virgil yesterday,
and many of them seemed to me crude enthusiasm, more like a
deafening shout, many of them. But one speech had range,
something of overstatement, something of statement, and something of understatement. It had all the colors of an enthusiasm
passed through an idea.

I would be willing to throw away everything else but that:
enthusiasm tamed by metaphor. Let me rest the case there. Enthusiasm tamed to metaphor, tamed to that much of it. I do not
think anybody ever knows the discreet use of metaphor, his
own and other people's, the discreet handling of metaphor, unless he has been properly educated in poetry.

Poetry begins in trivial metaphors, pretty metaphors, "grace"
metaphors, and goes on to the profoundest thinking that we
have. Poetry provides the one permissible way of saying one
thing and meaning another. People say, "Why don't you say
what you mean?" We never do that, do we, being all of us too

much poets. We like to talk in parables and in hints and in in-
directions—whether from diffidence or some other instinct.

I have wanted in late years to go further and further in making metaphor the whole of thinking. I find some one now and
then to agree with me that all thinking, except mathematical
thinking, is metaphorical, or all thinking except scientific thinking. The mathematical might be difficult for me to bring in, but
the scientific is easy enough.

Once on a time all the Greeks were busy telling each other
what the All was—or was like unto. All was three elements, air,
earth, and water (we once thought it was ninety elements; now
we think it is only one). All was substance, said another. All
was change, said a third. But best and most fruitful was Pythag-
oras' comparison of the universe with number. Number of
what? Number of feet, pounds, and seconds was the answer,
and we had science and all that has followed in science. The
metaphor has held and held, breaking down only when it came
to the spiritual and psychological or the out of the way places
of the physical.

The other day we had a visitor here, a noted scientist, whose
latest word to the world has been that the more accurately you
know where a thing is, the less accurately you are able to state
how fast it is moving. You can see why that would be so, without going back to Zeno's problem of the arrow's flight. In car-
rying numbers into the realm of space and at the same time into
the realm of time you are mixing metaphors, that is all, and you
are in trouble. They won't mix. The two don't go together.

Let's take two or three more of the metaphors now in use to
live by. I have just spoken of one of the new ones, a charming
mixed metaphor right in the realm of higher mathematics and
higher physics: that the more accurately you state where a thing
is, the less accurately you will be able to tell how fast it is mov-

ing. And, of course, everything is moving. Everything is an
event now. Another metaphor. A thing, they say, is an event.
Do you believe it is? Not quite. I believe it is almost an event.
But I like the comparison of a thing with an event.

I notice another from the same quarter. "In the neighborhood of matter space is something like curved." Isn't that a
good one! It seems to me that that is simply and utterly charming—to say that space is something like curved in the neighborhood of matter. "Something like."

Another amusing one is from—what is the book?—I can't
say it now; but here is the metaphor. Its aim is to restore you to
your ideas of free will. It wants to give you back your freedom
of will. All right, here it is on a platter. You know that you
can't tell by name what persons in a certain class will be dead
ten years after graduation, but you can tell actuarially how
many will be dead. Now, just so this scientist says of the particles of matter flying at a screen, striking a screen; you can't tell
what individual particles will come, but you can say in general
that a certain number will strike in a given time. It shows, you
see, that the individual particle can come freely. I asked Bohr
about that particularly, and he said, "Yes, it is so. It can come
when it wills and as it wills; and the action of the individual
particle is unpredictable. But it is not so of the action of the
mass. There you can predict." He says, "That gives the individual atom its freedom, but the mass its necessity."

Another metaphor that has interested us in our time and has
done all our thinking for us is the metaphor of evolution. Never
mind going into the Latin word. The metaphor is simply the
metaphor of the growing plant or of the growing thing. And
somebody very brilliantly, quite a while ago, said that the
whole universe, the whole of everything, was like unto a growing thing. That is all. I know the metaphor will break down at

some point, but it has not failed everywhere. It is a very brilliant metaphor, I acknowledge, though I myself get too tired of the kind of essay that talks about the evolution of candy, we will say, or the evolution of elevators—the evolution of this, that, and the other. Everything is evolution. I emancipate myself by simply saying that I didn't get up the metaphor and so am not much interested in it.

What I am pointing out is that unless you are at home in the metaphor, unless you have had your proper poetical education in the metaphor, you are not safe anywhere. Because you are not at ease with figurative values: you don't know the metaphor in its strength and its weakness. You don't know how far you may expect to ride it and when it may break down with you. You are not safe in science; you are not safe in history. In history, for instance—to show that [it] is the same in history as elsewhere—I heard somebody say yesterday that Aeneas was to be likened unto (those words, "likened unto"!) George Washington. He was that type of national hero, the middle-class man, not thinking of being a hero at all, bent on building the future, bent on his children, his descendants. A good metaphor, as far as it goes, and you must know how far. And then he added that Odysseus should be likened unto Theodore Roosevelt. I don't think that is so good. Someone visiting Gibbon at the point of death, said he was the same Gibbon as of old, still at his parallels.

Take the way we have been led into our present position morally, the world over. It is by a sort of metaphorical gradient. There is a kind of thinking—to speak metaphorically— there is a kind of thinking you might say was endemic in the brothel. It is always there. And every now and then in some mysterious way it becomes epidemic in the world. And how does it do so? By using all the good words that virtue has invented to maintain virtue. It uses honesty, first,—frankness, sincerity—those words; picks them up, uses them. "In the name of honesty, let us see what we are." You know. And then it picks up the word joy. "Let us in the name of joy, which is the enemy of our ancestors, the Puritans . . . Let us in the name of joy, which is the enemy of the kill-joy Puritan . . ." You see. "Let us," and so on. And then, "In the name of health . . ." Health is another good word. And that is the metaphor Freudianism trades on, mental health. And the first thing we know, it has us all in up to the top knot. I suppose we may blame the artists a good deal, because they are great people to spread by metaphor. The stage too—the stage is always a good intermediary between the two worlds, the under and the upper,—if I may say so without personal prejudice to the stage.

In all this I have only been saying that the devil can quote Scripture, which simply means that the good words you have lying around the devil can use for his purposes as well as anybody else. Never mind about my morality. I am not here to urge anything. I don't care whether the world is good or bad—not on any particular day.

Let me ask you to watch a metaphor breaking down here before you.

Somebody said to me a little while ago, "It is easy enough for me to think of the universe as a machine, as a mechanism."

I said, "You mean the universe is like a machine?"

He said, "No. I think it is one . . . Well, it is like . . ."

"I think you mean the universe is like a machine."

"All right. Let it go at that."

I asked him, "Did you ever see a machine without a pedal for the foot, or a lever for the hand, or a button for the finger?"

He said, "No—no."

I said, "All right. Is the universe like that?"

And he said, "No. I mean it is like a machine, only . . ."

". . . it is different from a machine," I said.

He wanted to go just that far with that metaphor and no further. And so do we all. All metaphor breaks down somewhere. That is the beauty of it. It is touch and go with the metaphor, and until you have lived with it long enough you don't know when it is going. You don't know how much you can get out of it and when it will cease to yield. It is a very living thing. It is as life itself.

I have heard this ever since I can remember, and ever since I have taught: the teacher must teach the pupil to think. I saw a teacher once going around in a great school and snapping pupils' heads with thumb and finger and saying, "Think." That was when thinking was becoming the fashion. The fashion hasn't yet quite gone out.

We still ask boys in college to think, as in the nineties, but we seldom tell them what thinking means; we seldom tell them it is just putting this and that together; it is just saying one thing in terms of another. To tell them is to set their feet on the first rung of a ladder the top of which sticks through the sky.

Greatest of all attempts to say one thing in terms of another is the philosophical attempt to say matter in terms of spirit, or spirit in terms of matter, to make the final unity. That is the greatest attempt that ever failed. We stop just short there. But it is the height of poetry, the height of all thinking, the height of all poetic thinking, that attempt to say matter in terms of spirit and spirit in terms of matter. It is wrong to call anybody a materialist simply because he tries to say spirit in terms of matter, as if that were a sin. Materialism is not the attempt to say all in terms of matter. The only materialist—be he poet, teacher, scientist, politician, or statesman—is the man who gets lost in his material without a gathering metaphor to throw it into shape and order. He is the lost soul.

We ask people to think, and we don't show them what thinking is. Somebody says we don't need to show them how

to think; bye and bye they will think. We will give them the
forms of sentences and, if they have any ideas, then they will
know how to write them. But that is preposterous. All there is
to writing is having ideas. To learn to write is to learn to have
ideas.

The first little metaphor . . . Take some of the trivial ones.
I would rather have trivial ones of my own to live by than the
big ones of other people.

I remember a boy saying, "He is the kind of person that
wounds with his shield." That may be a slender one, of course.
It goes a good way in character description. It has poetic grace.
"He is the kind that wounds with his shield."

The shield reminds me—just to linger a minute—the shield
reminds me of the inverted shield spoken of in one of the books
of the "Odyssey," the book that tells about the longest swim on
record. I forget how long it lasted—several days, was it?—but
at last as Odysseus came near the coast of Phaeacia, he saw it
on the horizon "like an inverted shield."

There is a better metaphor in the same book. In the end Odysseus comes ashore and crawls up the beach to spend the night
under a double olive tree, and it says, as in a lonely farmhouse
where it is hard to get fire—I am not quoting exactly—where
it is hard to start the fire again if it goes out, they cover the
seeds of fire with ashes to preserve it for the night, so Odysseus
covered himself with the leaves around him and went to sleep.
There you have something that gives you character, something
of Odysseus himself. "Seeds of fire." So Odysseus covered the
seeds of fire in himself. You get the greatness of his nature.

But these are slighter metaphors than the ones we live by.
They have their charm, their passing charm. They are as it were
the first steps toward the great thoughts, grave thoughts,
thoughts lasting to the end.

The metaphor whose manage we are best taught in poetry—
that is all there is of thinking. It may not seem far for the mind
to go but it is the mind's furthest. The richest accumulation of
the ages is the noble metaphors we have rolled up.

I want to add one thing more that the experience of poetry is
to anyone who comes close to poetry. There are two ways of
coming close to poetry. One is by writing poetry. And some
people think I want people to write poetry, but I don't; that is,
I don't necessarily. I only want people to write poetry if they
want to write poetry. I have never encouraged anybody to
write poetry that did not want to write it, and I have not always encouraged those who did want to write it. That ought to
be one's own funeral. It is a hard, hard life, as they say.

(I have just been to a city in the West, a city full of poets, a
city they have made safe for poets. The whole city is so lovely
that you do not have to write it up to make it poetry; it is
ready-made for you. But, I don't know—the poetry written in
that city might not seem like poetry if read outside of the city.
It would be like the jokes made when you were drunk; you
have to get drunk again to appreciate them.)

But as I say, there is another way to come close to poetry,
fortunately, and that is in the reading of it, not as linguistics, not
as history, not as anything but poetry. It is one of the hard
things for a teacher to know how close a man has come in reading poetry. How do I know whether a man has come close to
Keats in reading Keats? It is hard for me to know. I have lived
with some boys a whole year over some of the poets and I have
not felt sure whether they have come near what it was all about.
One remark sometimes told me. One remark was their mark
for the year; had to be—it was all I got that told me what I
wanted to know. And that is enough, if it was the right remark,
if it came close enough. I think a man might make twenty fool

remarks if he made one good one some time in the year. His mark would depend on that good remark.

The closeness—everything depends on the closeness with which you come, and you ought to be marked for the closeness, for nothing else. And that will have to be estimated by chance remarks, not by question and answer. It is only by accident that you know some day how near a person has come.

The person who gets close enough to poetry, he is going to know more about the word *belief* than anybody else knows, even in religion nowadays. There are two or three places where we know belief outside of religion. One of them is at the age of fifteen to twenty, in our self-belief. A young man knows more about himself than he is able to prove to anyone. He has no knowledge that anybody else will accept as knowledge. In his foreknowledge he has something that is going to believe itself into fulfilment, into acceptance.

There is another belief like that, the belief in someone else, a relationship of two that is going to be believed into fulfilment. That is what we are talking about in our novels, the belief of love. And the disillusionment that the novels are full of is simply the disillusionment from disappointment in that belief. That belief can fail, of course.

Then there is a literary belief. Every time a poem is written, every time a short story is written, it is written not by cunning, but by belief. The beauty, the something, the little charm of the thing to be, is more felt than known. There is a common jest, one that always annoys me, on the writers, that they write the last end first, and then work up to it; that they lay a train toward one sentence that they think is pretty nice and have all fixed up to set like a trap to close with. No, it should not be that way at all. No one who has ever come close to the arts has failed to see the difference between things written that way, with cunning and device, and the kind that are believed into existence, that begin in something more felt than known. This you can realize quite as well—not quite as well, perhaps, but nearly as well—in reading as you can in writing. I would undertake to separate short stories on that principle; stories that have been believed into existence and stories that have been cunningly devised. And I could separate the poems still more easily.

Now I think—I happen to think—that those three beliefs that I speak of, the self-belief, the love-belief, and the art-belief, are all closely related to the God-belief, that the belief in God is a relationship you enter into with Him to bring about the future.

There is a national belief like that, too. One feels it. I have been where I came near getting up and walking out on the people who thought that they had to talk against nations, against nationalism, in order to curry favor with internationalism. Their metaphors are all mixed up. They think that because a Frenchman and an American and an Englishman can all sit down on the same platform and receive honors together, it must be that there is no such thing as nations. That kind of bad thinking springs from a source we all know. I should want to say to anyone like that: "Look! First I want to be a person. And I want you to be a person, and then we can be as interpersonal as you please. We can pull each other's noses—do all sorts of things. But, first of all, you have got to have the personality. First of all, you have got to have the nations and then they can be as international as they please with each other."

I should like to use another metaphor on them. I want my palette, if I am a painter, I want my palette on my thumb or on my chair, all clean, pure, separate colors. Then I will do the mixing on the canvas. The canvas is where the work of art is, where we make the conquest. But we want the nations all separate, pure, distinct, things as separate as we can make them; and then in our thoughts, in our arts, and so on, we can do what we please about it.

But I go back. There are four beliefs that I know more about from having lived with poetry. One is the personal belief, which is a knowledge that you don't want to tell other people about because you cannot prove that you know. You are saying nothing about it till you see. The love belief, just the same, has that same shyness. It knows it cannot tell; only the outcome can tell. And the national belief we enter into socially with each other, all together, party of the first part, party of the second part, we enter into that to bring the future of the country. We cannot tell some people what it is we believe, partly, because they are too stupid to understand and partly because we are too proudly vague to explain. And anyway it has got to be fulfilled, and we are not talking until we know more, until we have something to show. And then the literary one in every work of art, not of cunning and craft, mind you, but of real art; that believing the thing into existence, saying as you go more than you even hoped you were going to be able to say, and coming with surprise to an end that you foreknew only with some sort of emotion. And then finally the relationship we enter into with God to believe the future in—to believe the hereafter in.

*"Maturity No Object"*

# "Maturity No Object"

MATURITY is no object except perhaps in education where you might think from all the talk the aim and end of everything was to get sophisticated before educated. Shakespeare says it is the right virtue of the medlar to be rotten before it is ripe. Overdevelop the social conscience and make us all social meddlers. But I digress before I begin. My theme is not education, but poetry and how young one has to be or stay to make it. And it is not schools in general I reflect on, only bad schools which something should be done about before they get much larger. My excuse is that school and poetry come so near being one thing. Poetry has been a great concern of school all down the ages. A large part of reading in school always has been and still is poetry; and it is but an extension from the metaphors of poetry out into all thinking, scientific and philosophic. In fact the poet and scholar have so much in common and live together so naturally that it is easy to make too much of a mystery about where they part company. Their material seems the

"Maturity No Object" was written as the introduction to an anthology of younger poets, published in 1957 with the title *New Poets of England and America.*

same—perhaps differs a little in being differently come by and differently held in play. Thoroughness is the danger of the scholar, dredging to the dregs. He works on assignment and self-assignment with some sense of the value of what he is getting when he is getting it. He is perhaps too avid of knowledge. The poet's instinct is to shun or shed more knowledge than he can swing or sing. His most available knowledge is acquired unconsciously. Something warns him dogged determination however profound can only result in doggerel. His danger is rhyming trivia. His depth is the lightsome blue depth of the air.

But I suppose the special distinction I was going to invest the poet with, that is making no object of maturity, was a mistake. It certainly belongs as much to the composer, the musician, the general, and I'm told the mathematician and the scientist. And it probably belongs to the scholar. Be that as it may, all poets I have ever heard of struck their note long before forty, the deadline for contributions to this book. The statistics are all in favor of their being as good and lyric as they will ever be. They may have ceased to be poets by the time appreciation catches up with them as Matthew Arnold complains somewhere. (I don't have to say exactly where because I'm not a scholar.) I have personal reasons to trust that they may go phasing on into being as good poets in their later mental ages. For my country's sake I might wish one or two of them an old age of epic writing. A good epic would grace our history. Landor has set an example in prolonging the lyric out of all bounds.

Maturity will come. We mature. But the point is that it is at best irrelevant. Young poetry is the breath of parted lips. For the spirit to survive, the mouth must find how to firm and not harden. I saw it in two faces in the same drawing room—one youth in Greek sculpture, the other manhood in modern painting. They were both noble. The man was no better than the boy nor worse because he was older. The poets of this group, many of them my friends and already known to many of us, need live to write no better, need only wait to be better known for what they have written. The reader is more on trial here than they are. He is given his chance to see if he can tell all by himself without critical instruction the difference between the poets who wrote because they thought it would be a good idea to write and those who couldn't help writing out of a strong weakness for the muse, as for an elopement with her. There should be some way to tell that just as there is to tell the excitement of the morning from the autointoxication of midnight. Any distinction between maturity and immaturity is not worth making unless as a precaution. If school is going to proclaim a policy of maturing boys and girls ultimately it might become necessary for us to stay away from school or at least play hooky a good deal to season slowly out of doors rather than in an oven or in a tanning vat. And that seems too bad; for so many of us like school and want to go there.

As I often say a thousand, two thousand, colleges, town and gown together in the little town they make, give us the best audiences for poetry ever had in all this world. I am in on the ambition that this book will get to them—heart and mind.

*"The Hear-Say Ballad"*

# "The Hear-Say Ballad"

"AN ordinary song or ballad that is the delight of the common people cannot fail to please all such readers as are not unqualified for the entertainment by their affectation or their ignorance."

Thus Addison with his challenge two hundred odd years ago and it might be Mrs. Flanders speaking today. We are defied not to love ballads on pain of being thought what Addison says. Balladry belongs to the none too literate and its spirit, and probably the spirit of all poetry, is safest in the keeping of the none too literate—people who know it by heart where it can weather and season properly. Ballads lead their life in the mouths and ears of men by hear-say like bluebirds and flickers in the nest holes of hollow trees. But that's no reason specimens shouldn't be brought to book now and then for sport and scholarship. We have a right to satisfy our curiosity as to what variants they may have been running wild into while our backs were turned. We can't touch their existence as a breed either to in-

In contributing this introduction to *Ballads Migrant in New England* by Helen Hartness Flanders and Marguerite Olney, published in 1953, Mr. Frost writes with charm and insight about the ballad—and indirectly about the roots of all poetry.

crease or destroy them. Nothing we do can. Trout have to be
killed carefully so as not to exterminate them; have even to be
fished out and multiplied artificially in captivity for restocking
their own brooks. Ballads are different. Child hunted them,
Mrs. Flanders hunts them; and they have the vitality to stay
game at large, not to say gamey. You won't see the ballads of
this book going back from here in print to alter the versions of
the singers they were found on. No patronage of ours will smile
them out of using "fee" for a rhyme word, "lily-white hands"
for beauty, and lords and ladies for goodness knows what away
off here three thousand miles across the ocean and after three
hundred years of democracy. Their singers ought in consistency
to be equally excited over the coronation and the inauguration
that are in conjunction this graceful year of nineteen hundred
and fifty-three.

One word more to speed the launching enterprise.

The voice and ear are left at a loss what to do with the ballad
until supplied with the tune it was written to go with. That
might be the definition of a true poem. A ballad does not or
should not supply its own way of being uttered. For tune it depends on the music—a good set score. Unsung it stays half-
lacking—as Mrs. Flanders knows full well. She has been at the
same pains to recruit singers to sing the ballads for her on the
stage as to collect the ballads. It is always interesting to watch
how lowly the thing may lapse and still be poetry for the right
people. It may flaw in meter, syntax, logic, and sense. It may
seem to be going to pieces, breaking up, but it is only the voice
breaks with emotion.

*Introduction to*
King Jasper

.

# Introduction to
## *King Jasper*

IT may come to the notice of posterity (and then again it may not) that this, our age, ran wild in the quest of new ways to be new. The one old way to be new no longer served. Science put it into our heads that there must be new ways to be new. Those tried were largely by subtraction—elimination. Poetry, for example, was tried without punctuation. It was tried without capital letters. It was tried without metric frame on which to measure the rhythm. It was tried without any

---

E. A. Robinson's poem *King Jasper* was published in 1935, shortly after his death. In this introduction to the book Mr. Frost makes it plain that he recognized Robinson's stature and appreciated his taste and skill. Frost here produces some of his most memorable prose. He ends the piece by quoting the last two lines of one of Robinson's best poems. The complete poem is eight lines long:

### THE DARK HILLS

Dark hills at evening in the west,
Where sunset hovers like a sound
Of golden horns that sang to rest
Old bones of warriors under ground,
Far now from all the bannered ways
Where flash the legions of the sun,
You fade—as if the last of days
Were fading, and all wars were done.

images but those to the eye; and a loud general intoning had to be kept up to cover the total loss of specific images to the ear, those dramatic tones of voice which had hitherto constituted the better half of poetry. It was tried without content under the trade name of poesie pure. It was tried without phrase, epigram, coherence, logic and consistency. It was tried without ability. I took the confession of one who had had deliberately to unlearn what he knew. He made a back-pedalling movement of his hands to illustrate the process. It was tried premature like the delicacy of unborn calf in Asia. It was tried without feeling or sentiment like murder for small pay in the underworld. These many things was it tried without, and what had we left? Still something. The limits of poetry had been sorely strained, but the hope was that the idea had been somewhat brought out.

Robinson stayed content with the old-fashioned way to be new. I remember bringing the subject up with him. How does a man come on his difference, and how does he feel about it when he first finds it out? At first it may well frighten him, as his difference with the Church frightened Martin Luther. There is such a thing as being too willing to be different. And what shall we say to people who are not only willing but anxious? What assurance have they that their difference is not insane, eccentric, abortive, unintelligible? Two fears should follow us through life. There is the fear that we shan't prove worthy in the eyes of someone who knows us at least as well as we know ourselves. That is the fear of God. And there is the fear of Man —the fear that men won't understand us and we shall be cut off from them.

We began in infancy by establishing correspondence of eyes with eyes. We recognized that they were the same feature and we could do the same things with them. We went on to the visible motion of the lips—smile answered smile; then cautiously, by trial and error, to compare the invisible muscles of the mouth and throat. They were the same and could make the same sounds. We were still together. So far, so good. From here on the wonder grows. It has been said that recognition in art is all. Better say correspondence is all. Mind must convince mind that it can uncurl and wave the same filaments of subtlety, soul convince soul that it can give off the same shimmers of eternity. At no point would anyone but a brute fool want to break off this correspondence. It is all there is to satisfaction; and it is salutary to live in the fear of its being broken off.

The latest proposed experiment of the experimentalists is to use poetry as a vehicle of grievances against the un-Utopian state. As I say, most of their experiments have been by subtraction. This would be by addition of an ingredient that latter-day poetry has lacked. A distinction must be made between griefs and grievances. Grievances are probably more useful than griefs. I read in a sort of Sunday-school leaflet from Moscow, that the grievances of Chekhov against the sordidness and dullness of his home-town society have done away with the sordidness and dullness of home-town society all over Russia. They were celebrating the event. The grievances of the great Russians of the last century have given Russia a revolution. The grievances of their great followers in America may well give us, if not a revolution, at least some palliative pensions. We must suffer them to put life at its ugliest and forbid them not, as we value our reputation for liberality.

I had it from one of the youngest lately: "Whereas we once thought literature should be without content, we now know it should be charged full of propaganda." Wrong twice, I told him. Wrong twice and of theory prepense. But he returned to his position after a moment out for reassembly: "Surely art can be considered good only as it prompts to action." How soon,

I asked him. But there is danger of undue levity in teasing the young. The experiment is evidently started. Grievances are certainly a power and are going to be turned on. We must be very tender of our dreamers. They may seem like picketers or members of the committee on rules for the moment. We shan't mind what they seem, if only they produce real poems.

But for me, I don't like grievances. I find I gently let them alone wherever published. What I like is griefs and I like them Robinsonianly profound. I suppose there is no use in asking, but I should think we might be indulged to the extent of having grievances restricted to prose if prose will accept the imposition, and leaving poetry free to go its way in tears.

Robinson was a prince of heartachers amid countless achers of another part. The sincerity he wrought in was all sad. He asserted the sacred right of poetry to lean its breast to a thorn and sing its dolefullest. Let weasels suck eggs. I know better where to look for melancholy. A few superficial irritable grievances, perhaps, as was only human, but these are forgotten in the depth of griefs to which he plunged us.

Grievances are a form of impatience. Griefs are a form of patience. We may be required by law to throw away patience as we have been required to surrender gold; since by throwing away patience and joining the impatient in one last rush on the citadel of evil, the hope is we may end the need of patience. There will be nothing left to be patient about. The day of perfection waits on unanimous social action. Two or three more good national elections should do the business. It has been similarly urged on us to give up courage, make cowardice a virtue, and see if that won't end war, and the need of courage. Desert religion for science, clean out the holes and corners of the residual unknown, and there will be no more need of religion. (Religion is merely consolation for what we don't know.) But suppose there was some mistake, and the evil stood siege, the war didn't end, and something remained unknowable. Our having disarmed would make our case worse than it had ever been before. Nothing in the latest advices from Wall Street, the League of Nations, or the Vatican incline me to give up my holdings in patient grief.

There were Robinson and I, it was years ago, and the place (near Boston Common) was the Place, as we liked afterward to call it, of Bitters, because it was with bitters, though without bitterness, we could sit there and look out on the welter of dissatisfaction and experiment in the world around us. It was too long ago to remember who said what, but the sense of the meeting was, we didn't care how arrant a reformer or experimentalist a man was if he gave us real poems. For ourselves, we should hate to be read for any theory upon which we might be supposed to write. We doubted any poem could persist for any theory upon which it might have been written. Take the theory that poetry in our language could be treated as quantitative, for example. Poems had been written in spite of it. And poems are all that matter. The utmost of ambition is to lodge a few poems where they will be hard to get rid of, to lodge a few irreducible bits where Robinson lodged more than his share.

For forty years it was phrase on phrase on phrase with Robinson, and every one the closest delineation of something that *is* something. Any poet, to resemble him in the least, would have to resemble him in that grazing closeness to the spiritual realities. If books of verse were to be indexed by lines first in importance instead of lines first in position, many of Robinson's poems would be represented several times over. This should be seen to. The only possible objection is that it could not be done by any mere hireling of the moment, but would have to be the work of someone who had taken his impressions freely before he had any notion of their use. A particular poem's being represented several times would only increase the chance of its being located.

The first poet I ever sat down with to talk about poetry was Ezra Pound. It was in London in 1913. The first poet we talked about, to the best of my recollection, was Edwin Arlington Robinson. I was fresh from America and from having read *The Town Down the River*. Beginning at that book, I have slowly spread my reading of Robinson twenty years backward and forward, about equally in both directions.

I remember the pleasure with which Pound and I laughed over the fourth "thought" in

> Miniver thought, and thought, and thought,
> And thought about it.

Three "thoughts" would have been "adequate" as the critical praise-word then was. There would have been nothing to complain of, if it had been left at three. The fourth made the intolerable touch of poetry. With the fourth, the fun began. I was taken out on the strength of our community of opinion here, to be rewarded with an introduction to Miss May Sinclair, who had qualified as the patron authority on young and new poets by the sympathy she had shown them in *The Divine Fire*.

There is more to it than the number of "thoughts." There is the way the last one turns up by surprise round the corner, the way the shape of the stanza is played with, the easy way the obstacle of verse is turned to advantage. The mischief is in it.

> One pauses half afraid
> To say for certain that he played—

a man as sorrowful as Robinson. His death was sad to those who knew him, but nowhere near as sad as the lifetime of poetry to which he attuned our ears. Nevertheless, I say his much-admired restraint lies wholly in his never having let grief go further than it could in play. So far shall grief go, so far shall philosophy go, so far shall confidences go, and no further. Taste may set the limit. Humor is a surer dependence.

> And once a man was there all night,
> Expecting something every minute.

I know what the man wanted of Old King Cole. He wanted the heart out of his mystery. He was the friend who stands at the end of a poem ready in waiting to catch you by both hands with enthusiasm and drag you off your balance over the last punctuation mark into more than you meant to say. "I understand the poem all right, but please tell me what is behind it?" Such presumption needs to be twinkled at and baffled. The answer must be, "If I had wanted you to know, I should have told you in the poem."

We early have Robinson's word for it:

> The games we play
> To fill the frittered minutes of a day
> Good glasses are to read the spirit through.

He speaks somewhere of Crabbe's stubborn skill. His own was a happy skill. His theme was unhappiness itself, but his skill was as happy as it was playful. There is that comforting thought for those who suffered to see him suffer. Let it be said at the risk of offending the humorless in poetry's train (for there are a few such): his art was more than playful; it was humorous.

The style is the man. Rather say the style is the way the man takes himself; and to be at all charming or even bearable, the way is almost rigidly prescribed. If it is with outer seriousness, it must be with inner humor. If it is with outer humor, it must be with inner seriousness. Neither one alone without the other under it will do. Robinson was thinking as much in his sonnet

on Tom Hood. One ordeal of Mark Twain was the constant
fear that his occluded seriousness would be overlooked. That
betrayed him into his two or three books of out-and-out seriousness.

Miniver Cheevy was long ago. The glint I mean has kept
coming to the surface of the fabric all down the years. Yesterday in conversation, I was using "The Mill." Robinson could
make lyric talk like drama. What imagination for speech in
"John Gorham"! He is at his height between quotation marks.

> The miller's wife had waited long,
>     The tea was cold, the fire was dead;
> And there might yet be nothing wrong
>     In how he went and what he said:
> "There are no millers any more,"
>     Was all that she had heard him say.

"There are no millers any more." It might be an edict of
some power against industrialism. But no, it is of wider application. It is a sinister jest at the expense of all investors of life or
capital. The market shifts and leaves them with a car-barn full
of dead trolley cars. At twenty I commit myself to a life of religion. Now, if religion should go out of fashion in twenty-five
years, there would I be, forty-five years old, unfitted for anything else and too old to learn anything else. It seems immoral
to have to bet on such high things as lives of art, business, or the
church. But in effect, we have no alternative. None but an all-
wise and all-powerful government could take the responsibility
of keeping us out of the gamble or of insuring us against loss
once we were in.

The guarded pathos of "Mr. Flood's Party" is what makes it
merciless. We are to bear in mind the number of moons listen-
ing. Two, as on the planet Mars. No less. No more ("No more,
sir; that will do"). One moon (albeit a moon, no sun) would

have laid grief too bare. More than two would have dissipated grief entirely and would have amounted to dissipation. The emotion had to be held at a point.

> He set the jug down slowly at his feet
> With trembling care, knowing that most things break;
> And only when assured that on firm earth
> It stood, as the uncertain lives of men
> Assuredly did not . . .

There twice it gleams. Nor is it lost even where it is perhaps lost sight of in the dazzle of all those golden girls at the end of "The Sheaves." Granted a few fair days in a world where not all days are fair.

> "Well, Mr. Flood, we have the harvest moon
> Again, and we may not have many more;
> The bird is on the wing, the poet says,
> And you and I have said it here before.
> Drink to the bird."

Poetry transcends itself in the playfulness of the toast.

Robinson has gone to his place in American literature and left his human place among us vacant. We mourn, but with the qualification that, after all, his life was a revel in the felicities of language. And not just to no purpose. None has deplored.

> The inscrutable profusion of the Lord
> Who shaped as one of us a thing

so sad and at the same time so happy in achievement. Not for me to search his sadness to its source. He knew how to forbid encroachment. And there is solid satisfaction in a sadness that is not just a fishing for ministration and consolation. Give us immedicable woes—woes that nothing can be done for—woes flat and final. And then to play. The play's the thing. Play's the thing. All virtue in "as if."

> As if the last of days
> Were fading and all wars were done.

As if they were. As if, as if!

*"The Poetry of Amy Lowell"*

# "The Poetry of Amy Lowell"

IT IS absurd to think
that the only way
to tell if a poem is lasting is to wait and see if it lasts. The right
reader of a good poem can tell the moment it strikes him that
he has taken an immortal wound—that he will never get over
it. That is to say, permanence in poetry as in love is perceived
instantly. It hasn't to await the test of time. The proof of a
poem is not that we have never forgotten it, but that we knew
at sight that we never could forget it. There was a barb to it and
a tocsin that we owned to at once. How often I have heard it
in the voice and seen it in the eyes of this generation that Amy
Lowell had lodged poetry with them to stay.

The most exciting movement in nature is not progress, advance, but expansion and contraction, the opening and shutting
of the eye, the hand, the heart, the mind. We throw our arms

---

Frost was not carried away by Amy Lowell's powerful personality nor by
her much-publicized poetry; he was not easily carried away by any fashion or
change in fashion. But in this tribute, which originally appeared in *The Christian Science Monitor* of May 16, 1925, under the title "The Poetry of Amy
Lowell," he shows his skill in praising her judiciously, if not warmly. At the
same time, he says some strong and sensible things about poetry and how to
tell the lasting from the things that will perish.

wide with a gesture of religion to the universe; we close them around a person. We explore and adventure for a while and then we draw in to consolidate our gains. The breathless swing is between subject matter and form. Amy Lowell was distinguished in a period of dilation when poetry, in the effort to include a larger material, stretched itself almost to the breaking of the verse. Little ones with no more apparatus than a tea-cup looked on with alarm. She helped make it stirring times for a decade to those immediately concerned with art and to many not so immediately.

The water in our eyes from her poetry is not warm with any suspicion of tears; it is water flung cold, bright and many-colored from flowers gathered in her formal garden in the morning. Her Imagism lay chiefly in images to the eye. She flung flowers and everything there. Her poetry was forever a clear resonant calling off of things seen.

*"A Romantic Chasm"*

# "A Romantic Chasm"

HAVING a book in London is not quite the same thing today as it was in 1913 when I had my first book there or anywhere—half a lifetime and two wars ago. To be sure by 1913 I had already had it from Kipling that I was hopelessly hedged from the elder earth with alien speech. But hearing then I heard not. I was young and heedless. My vitality shed discouragement as the well-oiled feathers of a healthy duck shed wetness. And to be merely hedged off was no great matter. What was a hedge to the poacher in my blood of a shiny night in the season of the year? It took an American, a friend, Henry L. Mencken, to rouse me to a sense of national differences. My pedantry would be poor and my desert small with the educated if I could pretend to look unscared into the gulf his great book has made to yawn between the American and English languages.

---

"A Romantic Chasm," written as the introduction to Mr. Frost's English edition *A Masque of Reason* (1948), is a curiously quirky, difficult piece of prose in which the poet plays with the differences between England, where he was first recognized, and his native land, towards which he felt so deep a loyalty. His great friendship for the English poet Edward Thomas, who died in the First World War, shines through the difficulties he apparently had in writing the preface.

I wish Edward Thomas (that poet) were here to ponder gulfs in general with me as in the days when he and I tired the sun with talking on the footpaths and stiles of Leddington and Ryton. I should like to ask him if it isn't true that the world is in parts and the separation of the parts as important as the connection of the parts. Isn't the great demand for good spacing? But now I do not know the number of his mansion to write him so much as a letter of inquiry. The mansions so many would probably be numberless. Then I must leave it to Jack Haines in Gloucester to tell me frankly if the gulf in word or idiom has been seriously widening since the night when to illustrate our talk about the internationality of ferns, he boosted me up a small cliff to see by matchlight a spleenwort he knew of there.

The Dea knows (as we still say in New England) I would go to any length short of idolatry to keep Great Britain within speaking, or at least shouting, distance of America in the trying times seen ahead. I might not care to go for a hero myself, but I could perhaps persuade some Mark Curtius of our race to leap into the gulf in the forum for me and close it as much as it was thought needful. Anyway I might be tempted to enlist with the forlorn hope who would sacrifice all the words in both languages except a very limited few we could agree on as meaning the same in both; only with the proviso that I should be drawn on the committee for vocabulary where I could hold out for certain favourites for my own use, such as *quackery* for remedies too unorthodox, *boustrophedon* for a more scientific eye-reading (if science is really in earnest about advancing the humanities), *ornery* for the old-fashioned colonial pronunciation of ordinary with only one accent. And there are other good words I should have to consult Ivor Brown about before giving them up. *Sursanure*, for instance, for the way my wounds heal after cruel criticism.

It is beyond idealism of mine to think of closing the gulf so tight as to embarrass the beneficiaries of it on either verge. The Mother Country will hardly deny having profited in several ways by American independence in business and government. May she profit more. For me I should hate to miss the chance for exotic charm my distance overseas might lend me. Charm may be too strong a word. Suppose American had got as far away from English as present day English is from Chaucerian, or at least Elizabethan; obviously my verse by being in American would automatically, without mental expense on my part, be raised to the rank of having to be annotated. It might be advertised as with glossary. It might be studied.

I should surely hesitate to squeeze the Atlantic out from between the two continents lest it should raise the tide too high for ports in the Pacific to adjust their wharves to the change.

But I mustn't talk myself entirely out of respect for the gulf. I don't doubt its awesome reality. Still I begin to wonder if it is anything more than a 'romantic chasm' of poetry and slang.

If that is a question, Phoebus replied (and touched my trembling ears), I can support you in your wild Coleridgian surmise. The estrangement in language is pretty much due to the very word-shift by metaphor you do your best to take part in daily so as to hold your closest friend off where you can 'entertain her always as a stranger'—with the freshness of a stranger. It often looks dangerously like aberration into a new dialect. But it is mostly back and forth in the same place like the jumping of a grasshopper whose day's work gets him nowhere. And even when it is a word-drift, which is a chain of word-shifts all in one direction, it is nothing but that an average ingenuity with figures of speech can be counted on to keep up with, or in half a jiffy overtake. You are both free peoples so used to your freedom that you are not interested in talking too much about

what you are free from. Your pride is in what you dare to take
liberties with, be it word, friend or institution. In the beginning
was the word, to be sure, very sure, and a solid basic comfort it
remains in situ, but the fun only begins with the spirited when
you treat the word as a point of many departures. There is risk
in the play. But if some of the company get lost in the excitement, charge it up to proving the truth of chapter and verse in
the Gospel according to Saint Mark, although the oracle speaking is Delphic. Remember the future of the world may depend
on your keeping in practice with each other's quips and figures.

*Preface to*
Memoirs of the Notorious
Stephen Burroughs

# Preface to
## *Memoirs of the Notorious Stephen Burroughs*

ℙELHAM, Massachusetts, may never have produced anything else; it had a large part in producing the *Memoirs of the Notorious Stephen Burroughs*—this good book; or at least in starting the author on the criminal career of which it is a record. I like setting up the claim for Pelham, because I once lived there or thereabouts. But it is the kind of town I should have wanted to magnify anyway, whether I had lived in it or not, just one high old street along a ridge, not much to begin with and every year beautifully less. The railroads have worked modern magic against it from away off in the valleys and the woods have pressed in upon it till now there is nothing left but the church where Burroughs preached his unsanctified sermons, a few houses (among them, possibly, the one where he preached the funeral sermon that began his undoing), and here and there a good mowing field of about the size of a tea-tray in the sky.

I was back there the other day looking for Burroughs, and I saw three great ghosts instead of one, Burroughs, the rogue,

---

This preface to an edition of the *Memoirs of the Notorious Stephen Burroughs* was published in 1924 and is, therefore, the earliest of the prose pieces here included. It is an introduction to an almost unknown but remarkable figure.

81

Glazier Wheeler, the coiner, and Daniel Shays, the rebel, a
shining company. Such places always have all their great men
at once, as if they were neither born nor self-made, but created
each other. I suppose I saw the three as they must have gotten
together to talk subversion of an evening at the Leanders'. Poor
old Shays! He was so scared by his own rebellion that once he
started running away from it, he never stopped till he got to
Sandgate, Vermont,—if you can imagine how far out of the
world that is—at any rate it was then outside of the United
States. Burroughs should have told us more about his Pelham
friends, and especially about Glazier Wheeler, who on his serious side was concerned with the transmutation of metals and
may have been a necromancer.

I was anxious to ask Burroughs if he wouldn't agree with me
that his own chief distinction was hypocrisy. Many will be satisfied to see in him just another specimen of the knowing rascal.
I choose to take it that he is here raised up again as an example
to us of the naïve hypocrite.

We assume that by virtue of being bad we are at least safe
from being hypocrites. But are we any such thing? We bad
people I should say had appearances to keep up no less dangerously than the good. The good must at all costs seem good; that
is the weakness of their position. But the bad must seem amiable
and engaging. They must often have to pass for large-hearted
when it is nothing but a strain on the heart that makes the heart
secretly sick. That is one curse that is laid on them; and another
is that in every out-and-out clash with the righteous they must
try to make themselves out more right than the righteous. You
can see what that would lead to. No, I am afraid hypocrisy is as
increasing to evil as it is diminishing to good.

I was not a church-goer at the time when Burroughs was
preaching in Pelham, and there may have been circumstances in

aggravation that he does not set down, but, let him tell it, I see little in the story to count against him. If the sermons were sound and the preacher able, it couldn't have mattered much that they were stolen and he not ordained. Technically, he was an impostor, and I suppose I am too inclined to be lenient with irregularity in both school and church. But I remember that Melchizedek was not a Levite and men have taught in colleges with no degree beyond a bachelor's. And take Burroughs' first serious lapse in attempting to pass counterfeit money in Springfield. Crime couldn't be made more excusable. Just one little dollar at a drugstore in the interests of scientific experiment and to save the tears of a lovely lady. I suspect he was not frank with us about what brought him sneaking back to Pelham after he was driven out with pitchforks. The friendship of the Leanders, was it? And equally that of Mr. and Mrs. Leander? And not at all the poetic young dream of easy money? The sweet hypocrite, we must never let him drop.

And couldn't he write, couldn't he state things? In his lifetime, he made the only two revolts from Puritanism anyone has yet thought of, one backwards into Paganism and the other, let us say, sideways into the Catholic Church. In making the first, he put the case for Paganism almost as well as Milton puts it in the mouth of the sorcerer Comus: "We that are of purer fire." How well he argues against holding anyone locked up in a jail in a free country, and in favor of free coining in a free country!

I should like to have heard his reasons for winding up in the Catholic Church. I can conceive of their being honest. Probably he was tired of his uncharted freedom out of jail and wanted to be moral and a Puritan again as when a child, but this time under a cover where he couldn't be made fun of by the intellectuals. The course might commend itself to the modern Puritan (what there is left of the modern Puritan).

Let me tell the reader where he must put this book if he will please me and why there. On the same shelf with Benjamin Franklin and Jonathan Edwards (grandfather of Aaron Burr). Franklin will be a reminder of what we have been as a young nation in some respects, Edwards in others. Burroughs comes in reassuringly when there is question of our not unprincipled wickedness, whether we have had enough of it for salt. The world knows we are criminal enough. We commit our share of blind and inarticulate murder, for instance. But sophisticated wickedness, the kind that knows its grounds and can twinkle, could we be expected to have produced so fine a flower in a pioneer state? The answer is that we had it and had it early in Stephen Burroughs (not to mention Aaron Burr). It is not just a recent publisher's importation from Europe.

Could anything recent be more teasing to our proper prejudices than the way Burroughs mixed the ingredients when he ran off on his travels? He went not like a fool with no thought for the future and nothing to his name but the horse between his legs. He took with him a pocketful of sermons stolen from his father, in one fell act combining prudence, a respect for religion (as property) and a respect for his father (as a preacher). *He* knew how to put the reverse on a ball so that when it was going it was also coming. It argues a sophisticated taste in the society around him that he should have found friends such as the Leanders to enjoy his jokes with him.

A book that I for one should be sorry to have missed. I have to thank my friend W. R. Brown for bringing it to my attention.

*"Perfect Day—
A Day of Prowess"*

# "Perfect Day—
# A Day of Prowess"

AMERICANS would rath-
er watch a game than play
a game. Statement true or false? Why, as to these thousands
here today to watch the game and not play it, probably not one
man-jack but has himself played the game in his athletic years
and got himself so full of bodily memories of the experience
(what we farmers used to call kinesthetic images) that he can
hardly sit still. We didn't burst into cheers immediately, but an
exclamation swept the crowd as if we felt it all over in our muscles when Boyer at third made the two impossible catches, one
a stab at a grounder and the other a leap at a line drive that may
have saved the day for the National League. We all winced
with fellow feeling when Berra got the foul tip on the ungloved
fingers of his throwing hand.

---

Robert Frost had a life-long interest in baseball. He was a pitcher in his youth;
he was still running bases in softball games on his farm in his seventies. He
knew baseball; he could talk baseball; and, characteristically, he always cared
very much about the score. In a letter to another poet, written in November of
1937, Frost says, ". . . and nothing flatters me more than to have it assumed
that I could write prose—unless it be to have it assumed that I once pitched
baseball with distinction." When, in 1956, he wrote this piece for *Sports Illustrated* he remarked, "It is the first time I have met a deadline since I was a re-
porter on the *Lawrence American* in 1894."

As for the ladies present, they are here as next friends to the men, but even they have many of them pitching arms and batting eyes. Many of them would prefer a league ball to a pumpkin. You wouldn't want to catch them with bare hands. I mustn't count it against them that I envision one in the outfield at a picnic with her arms spread wide open for a fly ball as for a descending man-angel. Luckily it didn't hit her in the mouth which was open too, or it might have hurt her beauty. It missed her entirely.

How do I know all this and with what authority do I speak? Have I not been written up as a pitcher in *The New Yorker* by the poet, Raymond Holden?—though the last full game I pitched in was on the grounds of Rockingham Park in Salem, New Hampshire, before it was turned into a race track. If I have shone at all in the all-star games at Breadloaf in Vermont it has been as a relief pitcher with a soft ball I despise like a picture window. Moreover I once took an honorary degree at Williams College along with a very famous pitcher, Ed Lewis, who will be remembered and found in the record to have led the National League in pitching quite a long time ago. His degree was not for pitching. Neither was mine. His was for presiding with credit over the University of New Hampshire and the Massachusetts College of Agriculture. He let me into the secret of how he could make a ball behave when his arm was just right. It may sound superstitious to the uninitiated, but he could push a cushion of air up ahead of it for it to slide off from any way it pleased. My great friendship for him probably accounts for my having made a trivial 10¢ bet on the National League today. He was a Welshman from Utica who, from having attended eisteddfods at Utica with his father, a bard, had like another Welsh friend of mine, Edward Thomas, in England, come to look on a poem as a performance one had to win. Chicago was my first favorite team because Chicago seemed the nearest city in the league to my original home town, San Francisco. I have conquered that prejudice. But I mean to see if the captain of it, Anson my boyhood hero, is in the Hall of Fame at Cooperstown where he belongs.

May I add to my self-citation that one of my unfulfilled promises on earth was to my fellow in art, Alfred Kreymborg, of an epic poem some day about a ball batted so hard by Babe Ruth that it never came back, but got to going round and round the world like a satellite. I got up the idea long before any artificial moon was thought of by the scientists. I meant to begin something like this:

> It was nothing to nothing at the end of the tenth
> And the prospects good it would last to the nth.

It needs a lot of work on it before it can take rank with *Casey at the Bat*.

In other words, some baseball is the fate of us all. For my part I am never more at home in America than at a baseball game like this in Clark Griffith's gem of a field, gem small, in beautiful weather in the capital of the country and my side winning. Here Walter Johnson flourished, who once threw a silver dollar across the Potomac (where not too wide) in emulation of George Washington, and here Gabby Street caught the bullet-like ball dropped from the top of George Washington's monument. It is the time and the place. And I have with me as consultant the well-known symbolist, Howard Schmitt of Buffalo, to mind my baseball slang and interpret the incidentals. The first player comes to the bat, Temple of the Redlegs, swinging two bats as he comes, the meaning of which or moral of which, I find on application to my consultant, is that we must always arrange to have just been doing something beforehand a good deal harder than what we are just going to do.

But when I asked him a moment later what it symbolized

when a ball got batted into the stands and the people instead of dodging in terror fought each other fiercely to get and keep it and were allowed to keep it, Howard bade me hold on; there seemed to be a misunderstanding between us. When he accepted the job it was orally; he didn't mean to represent himself as a symbolist in the high-brow or middle-brow sense of the word, that is as a collegiate expounder of the double entendre for college classes; he was a common ordinary cymbalist in a local band somewhere out on the far end of the Eeryie Canal. We were both honest men. He didn't want to be taken for a real professor any more than I wanted to be taken for a real sport. His utmost wish was to contribute to the general noise when home runs were made. He knew they would be the most popular hits of the day. And they were—four of them from exactly the four they were expected from, Musial, Williams, Mays and Mantle. The crowd went wild four times. Howard's story would have been more plausible if he had brought his cymbals with him. I saw I would have to take care of the significances myself. This comes of not having got it in writing. The moral is always get it in writing.

Time was when I saw nobody on the field but the players. If I saw the umpire at all it was as an enemy for not taking my side. I may never have wanted to see bottles thrown at him so that he had to be taken out by the police. Still I often regarded him with the angry disfavor that the Democratic Party showed the Supreme Court in the '30s and other parties have shown it in other crises in our history. But now grown psychological, shading 100, I saw him as a figure of justice, who stood forth alone to be judged as a judge by people and players with whom he wouldn't last a week if suspected of the least lack of fairness or the least lack of faith in the possibility of fairness. I was touched by his loneliness and glad it was relieved a little by his being five in number, five in one so to speak, *e pluribus unum*. I have it from high up in the judiciary that some justices see in him an example to pattern after. Right there in front of me for reassurance is the umpire brought up perhaps in the neighborhood of Boston who can yet be depended upon not to take sides today for or against the American League the Boston Red Sox belong to. Let me celebrate the umpire for any influence for the better he may have on the Supreme Court. The justices suffer the same predicaments with him. I saw one batter linger perceptibly to say something to the umpire for calling him out on a third strike. I didn't hear what the batter said. One of the hardest things to accept as just is a called third strike.

It has been a day of prowess in spite of its being a little on the picnic side and possibly not as desperately fought as it might be in a World Series. Prowess, prowess, in about equal strength for both sides. Each team made 11 hits, two home runs and not a single error. The day was perfect, the scene perfect, the play perfect. Prowess of course comes first, the ability to perform with success in games, in the arts and, come right down to it, in battle. The nearest of kin to the artists in college where we all become bachelors of arts are their fellow performers in baseball, football and tennis. That's why I am so particular college athletics should be kept from corruption. They are close to the soul of culture. At any rate the Greeks thought so. Justice is a close second to prowess. When displayed toward each other by antagonists in war and peace, it is known as the nobility of noble natures. And I mustn't forget courage, for there is neither prowess nor justice without it. My fourth, if it is important enough in comparison to be worth bringing in, is knowledge, the mere information we can't get too much of and can't ever get enough of, we complain, before going into action.

As I say, I never feel more at home in America than at a ball game be it in park or in sandlot. Beyond this I know not. And dare not.

*"The Prerequisites"*

# "The Prerequisites"

$\mathcal{S}$OME sixty years ago a young reader ran into serious trouble with the blind last stanza of a poem otherwise perfectly intelligible. The interest today might be in what he then did about it. He simply left it to shift for itself. He might see to it if he ever saw it again. He guessed he was no more anxious to understand the poem than the poem was to be understood.

He might have gone to college for help. But he had just left college to improve his mind if he had any. Or he might have gone to Asia. The whole poem smacked of Asia. He suspected a whole religion behind it different from the one he was brought up to. But as he was no traveler except on foot he must have gone by way of the Bering Strait when frozen over and that might have taken him an epoch from East to West as it had the Indians from West to East.

The poem was called "Brahma" and he was lilting along on such lines as the following in easy recognition:

---

There is an abstract quality to the essay called "The Prerequisites." It was written for use as the preface to Mr. Frost's collection *Aforesaid*, published on his birthday in 1954, and originally appeared in *The New York Times Book Review* for March twenty-first of that year.

> They reckon ill who leave me out
> When me they fly I am the wings.
> I am the doubter and the doubt
> And I the hymn the Brahmin sings.

which was all very pretty. For Brahma he naturally read God
—not the God of the Old Testament nor of the New either,
but near enough. Though no special liberal he valued himself
on his tolerance of heresy in great thinkers. He could always
lend himself to an unsound idea for the duration of the piece
and had been even heard to wish people would cling to their
heresies long enough for him to go and tell on them.

Success in taking figures of speech is as intoxicating as success
in making figures of speech. It had to be just when he was
flushed with having held his own with the poem so far and was
thinking "good easy man" "What a good boy am I" that the
disaster happened. The words were still Brahma's:

> The strong gods pine for my abode
> And pine in vain the sacred seven
> But thou meek lover of the good
> Find me and turn thy back on Heaven.

There he blacked out as if he had bumped his head and he
only came to dazed. I remember his anger in asking if anybody
had a right to talk like that. But he wasn't as put out as he let on
to be. He didn't go back on poetry for more than the particular
poem or on that for more than the time being. His subconscious
intention was to return on it by stealth some day if only it
would stay in print till he was ready for it. All was he didn't
want the wrong kind of help. The heart sinks when robbed of
the chance to see for itself what a poem is all about. Any im-
mediate preface is like cramming the night before an examina-
tion. Too late, too late! Any footnote while the poem is going
is too late. Any subsequent explanation is as dispiriting as the
explanation of a joke. Being taught poems reduces them to the

rank of mere information. He was sure the Muse would thank him for reserving a few of her best for being achieved on the spur of the moment.

Approach to the poem must be from afar off, even generations off. He should close in on it on converging lines from many directions like the divisions of an army upon a battlefield.

A poem is best read in the light of all the other poems ever written. We read A the better to read B (we have to start somewhere; we may get very little out of A). We read B the better to read C, C the better to read D, D the better to go back and get something more out of A. Progress is not the aim, but circulation. The thing is to get among the poems where they hold each other apart in their places as the stars do.

And if he stubbornly stayed away from college and Asia (he hated to be caught at his age grooming his brains in public) perhaps in time college and Asia, even the Taj Mahal, might come to him with the prerequisites to that poem and to much else not yet clear.

Well, it so happened. For the story has a happy ending. Not fifty years later when the poem turned up again he found himself in a position to deal with all but two lines of it. He was not quite satisfied that the reference to "strong gods," plural, was fair poetry practice. Were these Titans or Yidags or, perish the thought, Olympians?—Oh no! not Olympians. But he now saw through the "meek lover of the good" who sounded so deceptively Christian. His meekness must have meant the perfect detachment from ambition and desire that can alone rescue us from the round of existence. And the "me" worth turning "thy back on Heaven" for must of course be Nirvana—the only nothing that is something. He had grown very fastidious about not calling the round of existence a wheel. He was a confirmed symbolist.

*Remarks Accepting*
*the Gold Medal of the*
*National Institute of*
*Arts and Letters*

# Remarks Accepting
# the Gold Medal of the
# National Institute of
# Arts and Letters

"HAVE you ever thought about rewards," I was asked lately in a tone of fear for me that I might not have thought at my age. I don't know what I was supposed to think, unless it was that the greatest reward of all was self-esteem. Saints, like John Bunyan, are all right in jail if they are sure of their truth and sincerity. But, so, also, are many criminals. The great trouble is to be sure. A stuffed shirt is the opposite of a criminal. He cares not what he thinks of himself so long as the world continues to think well of him. The sensible and healthy live somewhere between self-approval and the approval of society. They make their adjustment without too much talk of compromise.

Still an artist, however well he may fare, within and without, must often feel he has to rely too heavily on self-appraisal for comfort. For twenty years the world neglected him; then for twenty years it entreated him kindly. He has to take the respon-

---

In 1939 Mr. Frost was awarded the gold medal of the National Institute of Arts and Letters. These remarks were written out after the actual ceremony. He always regarded the Institute's medal as one of the greatest of all the prizes he received. His acceptance was published in volume five of the *National Institute News Bulletin*.

sibility of deciding when the world was wrong. He can't help wishing there was some third more disinterested party, such as God, or Time, to give absolute judgment.

Oh Time whose verdicts mock our own
The only righteous judge art thou.

The scientist seems to have the advantage of him in a court of larger appeal. A planet is perturbed in its orbit. The scientist stakes his reputation on the perturber's being found at a certain point in the sky at a certain time of night. All telescopes are turned that way, and sure enough, there the perturber is as bright as a button. The scientist knows he is good without being told. He has a mind and he has instruments, the extensions of mind that fit closely into the nature of the Universe. It is the same when an engineer has plotted two shafts to meet under the middle of a mountain and make a tunnel. The shafts approach each other; the workmen in one can hear the pickaxes of the workmen in the other. A sudden gleam of pickaxe breaks through. A human face shows in the face of the rock. The engineer is justified of his figures. He knows he has a mind. It has fitted into the nature of the Universe.

I should be sorry to concede the artist has no such recourse to tests of certainty at all. His hope must be that his work will prove to have fitted into the nature of people. Beyond my belief in myself, beyond another's critical opinion of me, lies this. I should like to have it that your medal is a token of my having fitted, not into the nature of the Universe, but in some small way, at least, into the nature of Americans—into their affections, is perhaps what I mean. I trust you will be willing to indulge me here and let me have it so for the occasion. But whatever the medal may or may not symbolize, I take it as a very great honor.

*Letter to*
The Amherst Student

# Letter to
## *The Amherst Student*

IT IS very, very kind of the *Student* to be showing sympathy with me for my age. But sixty is only a pretty good age. It is not advanced enough. The great thing is to be advanced. Now ninety would be really well along and something to be given credit for.

But speaking of ages, you will often hear it said that the age of the world we live in is particularly bad. I am impatient of such talk. We have no way of knowing that this age is one of the worst in the world's history. Arnold claimed the honor for the age before this. Wordsworth claimed it for the last but one. And so on back through literature. I say they claimed the honor for their ages. They claimed it rather for themselves. It is immodest of a man to think of himself as going down before the worst forces ever mobilized by God.

All ages of the world are bad—a great deal worse anyway than Heaven. If they weren't the world might just as well be

Mr. Frost's memorable letter to *The Amherst Student* appeared in the undergraduate newspaper of Amherst College on March 25, 1935. It was written in reply to a message of congratulation to him on his sixtieth birthday. The poet nowhere made a plainer statement of religious belief or philosophical position than in this little-known and most important document.

Heaven at once and have it over with. One can safely say after from six to thirty thousand years of experience that the evident design is a situation here in which it will always be about equally hard to save your soul. Whatever progress may be taken to mean, it can't mean making the world any easier a place in which to save your soul—or if you dislike hearing your soul mentioned in open meeting, say your decency, your integrity.

Ages may vary a little. One may be a little worse than another. But it is not possible to get outside the age you are in to judge it exactly. Indeed it is as dangerous to try to get outside of anything as large as an age as it would be to engorge a donkey. Witness the many who in the attempt have suffered a dilation from which the tissues and the muscles of the mind have never been able to recover natural shape. They can't pick up anything delicate or small any more. They can't use a pen. They have to use a typewriter. And they gape in agony. They can write huge shapeless novels, huge gobs of raw sincerity bellowing with pain and that's all that they can write.

Fortunately we don't need to know how bad the age is. There is something we can always be doing without reference to how good or how bad the age is. There is at least so much good in the world that it admits of form and the making of form. And not only admits of it, but calls for it. We people are thrust forward out of the suggestions of form in the rolling clouds of nature. In us nature reaches its height of form and through us exceeds itself. When in doubt there is always form for us to go on with. Anyone who has achieved the least form to be sure of it, is lost to the larger excruciations. I think it must stroke faith the right way. The artist[,] the poet[,] might be expected to be the most aware of such assurance. But it is really everybody's sanity to feel it and live by it. Fortunately, too, no forms are more engrossing[,] gratifying, comforting, staying than those lesser ones we throw off, like vortex rings of smoke, all our individual enterprise and needing nobody's co-operation; a basket, a letter, a garden, a room, an idea, a picture, a poem. For these we haven't to get a team together before we can play.

The background in hugeness and confusion shading away from where we stand into black and utter chaos; and against the background any small man-made figure of order and concentration. What pleasanter than that this should be so? Unless we are novelists or economists we don't worry about this confusion; we look out on [it] with an instrument or tackle it to reduce it. It is partly because we are afraid it might prove too much for us and our blend of democratic-republican-socialist-communist-anarchist party. But it is more because we like it, we were born to it, born used to it and have practical reasons for wanting it there. To me any little form I assert upon it is velvet, as the saying is, and to be considered for how much more it is than nothing. If I were a Platonist I should have to consider it, I suppose, for how much less it is than everything.

*"On Emerson"*

# "On Emerson"

ALL that admiration for me I am glad of. I am here out of admiration for Emerson and Thoreau. Naturally on this proud occasion I should like to make myself as much of an Emersonian as I can. Let me see if I can't go a long way. You may be interested to know that I have right here in my pocket a little first edition of Emerson's poetry. His very first was published in England, just as was mine. His book was given me on account of that connection by Fred Melcher, who takes so much pleasure in bringing books and things together like that.

I suppose I have always thought I'd like to name in verse some day my four greatest Americans: George Washington, the general and statesman; Thomas Jefferson, the political thinker; Abraham Lincoln, the martyr and savior; and fourth, Ralph Waldo Emerson, the poet. I take these names because they are

Nearly a quarter of a century after his letter to *The Amherst Student*, Mr. Frost in this piece touches again some of the same depths of belief and disbelief. To have these two pieces of prose together in one volume seems reason enough for the present book—even if there were no other reasons. Originally delivered as an address at the American Academy of Arts and Sciences, on the occasion of the award to Mr. Frost of the Emerson-Thoreau Medal, "On Emerson" was published in revised form in *Dædalus* in the fall of 1959.

going around the world. They are not just local. Emerson's name has gone as a poetic philosopher or as a philosophical poet, my favorite kind of both.

I have friends it bothers when I am accused of being Emersonian, that is, a cheerful Monist, for whom evil does not exist, or if it does exist, needn't last forever. Emerson quotes Burns as speaking to the Devil as if he could mend his ways. A melancholy dualism is the only soundness. The question is: is soundness of the essence.

My own unsoundness has a strange history. My mother was a Presbyterian. We were here on my father's side for three hundred years but my mother was fresh a Presbyterian from Scotland. The smart thing when she was young was to be reading Emerson and Poe as it is today to be reading St. John Perse or T. S. Eliot. Reading Emerson turned her into a Unitarian. That was about the time I came into the world; so I suppose I started a sort of Presbyterian-Unitarian. I was transitional. Reading on into Emerson, that is into "Representative Men" until she got to Swedenborg, the mystic, made her a Swedenborgian. I was brought up in all three of these religions, I suppose. I don't know whether I was baptized in them all. But as you see it was pretty much under the auspices of Emerson. It was all very Emersonian. Phrases of his began to come to me early. In that essay on the mystic he makes Swedenborg say that in the highest heaven nothing is arrived at by dispute. Everybody votes in heaven but everybody votes the same way, as in Russia today. It is only in the second-highest heaven that things get parliamentary; we get the two-party system or the hydra-headed, as in France.

Some of my first thinking about my own language was certainly Emersonian. "Cut these sentences and they bleed," he says. I am not submissive enough to want to be a follower, but he had me there. I never got over that. He came pretty near making me an anti-vocabularian with the passage in "Monadnock" about our ancient speech. He blended praise and dispraise of the country people of New Hampshire. As an abolitionist he was against their politics. Forty per cent of them were states-rights Democrats in sympathy with the South. They were really pretty bad, my own relatives included.

> The God who made New Hampshire
> Taunted the lofty land
> With little men;—

And if I may be further reminiscent parenthetically, my friend Amy Lowell hadn't much use for them either. "I have left New Hampshire," she told me. Why in the world? She couldn't stand the people. What's the matter with the people? "Read your own books and find out." They really differ from other New Englanders, or did in the days of Franklin Pierce.

But now to return to the speech that was his admiration and mine in a burst of poetry in "Monadnock":

> Yet wouldst thou learn our ancient speech
> These the masters that can teach.
> Fourscore or a hundred words
> All their vocal muse affords.
> Yet they turn them in a fashion
> Past the statesman's art and passion.
> Rude poets of the tavern hearth
> Squandering your unquoted mirth,
> That keeps the ground and never soars,
> While Jake retorts and Reuben roars.
> Scoff of yeoman, strong and stark,
> Goes like bullet to the mark,
> And the solid curse and jeer
> Never balk the waiting ear.

Fourscore or a hundred is seven hundred less than my friend Ivor Richard's basic eight hundred. I used to climb on board a

load of shooks (boxes that haven't been set up) just for the
pleasure I had in the driver's good use of his hundred-word
limit. This at the risk of liking it so much as to lose myself in
mere picturesqueness. I was always in favor of the solid curse as
one of the most beautiful of figures. We were warned against it
in school for its sameness. It depends for variety on the tones of
saying it and the situations.

I had a talk with John Erskine, the first time I met him, on
this subject of sentences that may look tiresomely alike, short
and with short words, yet turn out as calling for all sorts of
ways of being said aloud or in the mind's ear, Horatio. I took
Emerson's prose and verse as my illustration. Writing is un-
boring to the extent that it is dramatic.

In a recent preface to show my aversion to being interrupted
with notes in reading a poem, I find myself resorting to Emerson again. I wanted to be too carried away for that. There was
much of "Brahma" that I didn't get to begin with but I got
enough to make me sure I would be back there reading it again
some day when I had read more and lived more; and sure
enough, without help from dictionary or encyclopaedia I can
now understand every line in it but one or two. It is a long story
of many experiences that let me into the secret of:

> But thou, meek lover of the good!
> Find me, and turn thy back on heaven.

What baffled me was the Christianity in "meek lover of the
good." I don't like obscurity and obfuscation, but I do like dark
sayings I must leave the clearing of to time. And I don't want to
be robbed of the pleasure of fathoming depths for myself. It
was a moment for me when I saw how Shakespeare set bounds
to science when he brought in the North Star, "whose worth's
unknown although his height be taken." Of untold worth: it
brings home some that should and some that shouldn't come.

Let the psychologist take notice how unsuccessful he has to be.
I owe more to Emerson than anyone else for troubled thoughts
about freedom. I had the hurt to get over when I first heard us
made fun of by foreigners as the land of the free and the home
of the brave. Haven't we won freedom? Is there no such thing
as freedom? Well, Emerson says God

> Would take the sun out of the skies
> Ere freedom out of a man.

and there rings the freedom I choose.

Never mind how and where Emerson disabused me of my
notion I may have been brought up to that the truth would
make me free. My truth will bind you slave to me. He didn't
want converts and followers. He was a Unitarian. I am on record as saying that freedom is nothing but departure—setting
forth—leaving things behind, brave origination of the courage
to be new. We may not want freedom. But let us not deceive
ourselves about what we don't want. Freedom is one jump
ahead of formal laws, as in planes and even automobiles right
now. Let's see the law catch up with us very soon.

Emerson supplies the emancipating formula for giving an
attachment up for an attraction, one nationality for another
nationality, one love for another love. If you must break free,

> Heartily know,
> When half-gods go
> The gods arrive.

I have seen it invoked in *Harper's Magazine* to excuse disloyalty
to our democracy in a time like this. But I am not sure of the
reward promised. There is such a thing as getting too tran-
scended. There are limits. Let's not talk socialism. I feel projected out from politics with lines like:

> Musketaquit, a goblin strong,
> Of shards and flints makes jewels gay;
> They lose their grief who hear his song,
> And where he winds is the day of day.
>
> So forth and brighter fares my stream,—
> Who drink it shall not thirst again;
> No darkness stains its equal gleam,
> And ages drop in it like rain.

Left to myself, I have gradually come to see what Emerson was meaning in "Give all to Love" was, Give all to Meaning. The freedom is ours to insist on meaning.

The kind of story Steinbeck likes to tell is about an old labor hero punch-drunk from fighting the police in many strikes, beloved by everybody at headquarters as the greatest living hater of tyranny. I take it that the production line was his grievance. The only way he could make it mean anything was to try to ruin it. He took arms and fists against it. No one could have given him that kind of freedom. He saw it as his to seize. He was no freedman; he was a free man. The one inalienable right is to go to destruction in your own way. What's worth living for is worth dying for. What's worth succeeding in is worth failing in.

If you have piled up a great rubbish heap of oily rags in the basement for your doctor's thesis and it won't seem to burst into flame spontaneously, come away quickly and without declaring rebellion. It will cost you only your Ph.D. union card and the respect of the union. But it will hardly be noticed even to your credit in the world. All you have to do is to amount to something anyway. The only reprehensible materiality is the materialism of getting lost in your material so you can't find out yourself what it is all about.

A young fellow came to me to complain of the department of philosophy in his university. There wasn't a philosopher in

it. "I can't stand it." He was really complaining of his situation.
He wasn't where he could feel real. But I didn't tell him so I
didn't go into that. I agreed with him that there wasn't a philosopher in his university—there was hardly ever more than
one at a time in the world—and I advised him to quit. Light
out for somewhere. He hated to be a quitter. I told him the
Bible says, "Quit ye, like men." "Does it," he said. "Where
would I go?" Why anywhere almost. Kamchatka, Madagas-
car, Brazil. I found him doing well in the educational department of Rio when I was sent on an errand down there by our
government several years later. I had taken too much responsibility for him when I sent him glimmering like that. I wrote to
him with troubled conscience and got no answer for two whole
years. But the story has a happy ending. His departure was not
suicidal. I had a post card from him this Christmas to tell me he
was on Robinson Crusoe's island Juan Fernandez on his way to
Easter Island that it had always been a necessity for him some
day to see. I would next hear from him in Chile where he was
to be employed in helping restore two colleges. Two! And the
colleges were universities!

No subversive myself, I think it very Emersonian of me that
I am so sympathetic with subversives, rebels, runners out, runners out ahead, eccentrics, and radicals. I don't care how ex-
treme their enthusiasm so long as it doesn't land them in the
Russian camp. I always wanted one of them teaching in the
next room to me so my work would be cut out for me warning
the children taking my courses not to take his courses.

I am disposed to cheat myself and others in favor of any poet
I am in love with. I hear people say the more they love anyone
the more they see his faults. Nonsense. Love is blind and should
be left so. But it hasn't been hidden in what I have said that I
am not quite satisfied with the easy way Emerson takes dis-

loyalty. He didn't know or ignored his Blackstone. It is one thing for the deserter and another for the deserted. Loyalty is that for the lack of which your gang will shoot you without benefit of trial by jury. And serves you right. Be as treacherous as you must be for your ideals, but don't expect to be kissed good-by by the idol you go back on. We don't want to look too foolish, do we? And probably Emerson was too Platonic about evil. It was a mere Τὸ μὴ οὔ that could be disposed of like the butt of a cigarette. In a poem I have called the best Western poem yet he says:

> Unit and universe are round.

Another poem could be made from that, to the effect that ideally in thought only is a circle round. In practice, in nature, the circle becomes an oval. As a circle it has one center—Good. As an oval it has two centers—Good and Evil. Thence Monism versus Dualism.

Emerson was a Unitarian because he was too rational to be superstitious and too little a storyteller and lover of stories to like gossip and pretty scandal. Nothing very religious can be done for people lacking in superstition. They usually end up abominable agnostics. It takes superstition and the prettiest scandal story of all to make a good Trinitarian. It is the first step in the descent of the spirit into the material-human at the risk of the spirit.

But if Emerson had left us nothing else he would be remembered longer than the Washington Monument for the monument at Concord that he glorified with lines surpassing any other ever written about soldiers:

> By the rude bridge that arched the flood
> Their flag to April's breeze unfurled
> Here once the embattled farmers stood
> And fired the shot heard round the world.

Not even Thermopylae has been celebrated better. I am not a shriner, but two things I never happen on unmoved: one, this poem on stone; and the other, the tall shaft seen from Lafayette Park across the White House in Washington.